Discovering Prehistoric Animals

Written by Janet Craig

Illustrated by James Watling

Troll Associates

Library of Congress Cataloging-in-Publication Data

Discovering prehistoric animals / by Janet Craig; illustrated by
James Watling.
        p.   cm.
    Summary: Describes discoveries made by paleontologists regarding
how dinosaurs looked and lived millions of years ago.
    ISBN 0-8167-1755-9 (lib. bdg.)   ISBN 0-8167-1756-7 (pbk.)
    1. Dinosaurs—Juvenile literature.   [1. Dinosaurs.]   I. Watling,
James, ill.   II. Title.
QE862.D5P137   1990
567.91—dc20   89-4973

4.95

Let's go on a trip back in time. We'll travel back more than 65 million years—to a time when the earth was much younger.

The land and oceans were much different than they are today. Who lived on the open plains and in the forests, warm swamps and seas of so long ago? The dinosaurs and other prehistoric animals!

The word *dinosaur* means "terrible lizard." Although some of them looked a bit like giant lizards, the dinosaurs were not really lizards.

Dinosaurs were reptiles. The only reptiles alive today are snakes, turtles, lizards, and animals in the crocodile family. But none of these reptiles are closely related to the dinosaurs. In their time, though, the dinosaurs were found almost everywhere on earth.

These strange creatures lived for about 150 million years.

The Age of Dinosaurs was filled with odd-looking creatures. They came in many sizes and shapes. Some dinosaurs were giants. In fact, dinosaurs were the largest creatures ever to have lived on land.

Certain dinosaurs were fierce fighters. Their enormous heads were as long as a man. Their jaws were lined with long, sharp teeth.

Other dinosaurs were very long and heavy. Apatosaurus, also known as Brontosaurus, was one such giant. He weighed up to 40 tons and was more than 70 feet long. His thick, round legs were the size of tree trunks. Did the earth shake and thunder as Apatosaurus moved about? The person who named this creature Brontosaurus, not knowing it was already named Apatosaurus, certainly thought so, for *Brontosaurus* means "thunder lizard."

But not all dinosaurs were giants. One of the smallest was
Compsognathus. He was about the size of a chicken and
probably weighed only six pounds.

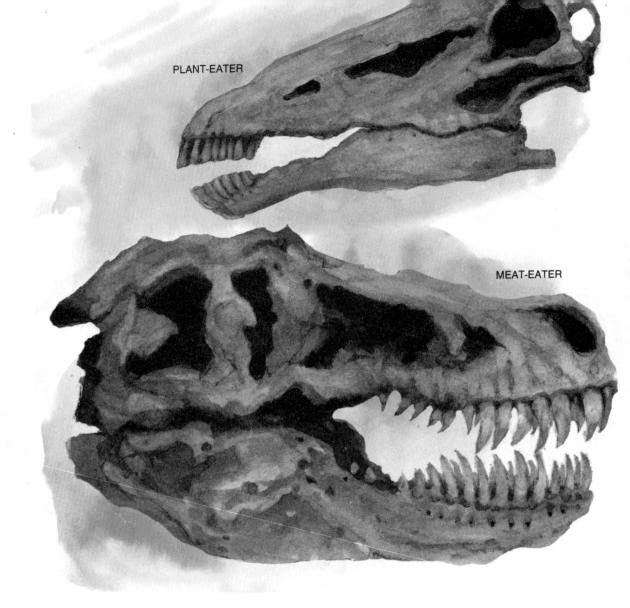

PLANT-EATER

MEAT-EATER

Some dinosaurs ate plants. Many of these animals had flat teeth for crushing and grinding their food. Some didn't have any grinding teeth at all, so they swallowed their food whole! Other dinosaurs were meat-eaters. They had sharp, pointed teeth for fighting and for tearing the flesh of their victims.

One ferocious meat-eater was Allosaurus. He lived about
140 million years ago. Walking on his two hind legs, Allosaurus
hunted in the warm, wet swamps for his dinner. This killer had
short front legs. At the end of each leg grew three sharp claws.
Allosaurus used his claws for holding his prey. The mouth of
Allosaurus was lined with knife-like teeth. They came in handy
for biting huge chunks of flesh. Many scientists think Allosaurus
attacked slow-moving dinosaurs such as Apatosaurus and
Stegosaurus.

Brachiosaurus was a gentle giant. He was one of the heaviest dinosaurs ever to have lived, weighing 70 tons or more. That is about as much as fifteen elephants!

Brachiosaurus, like other giant plant-eaters of his time, walked on all four legs. His head was small, but his neck was very long. This dinosaur's back sloped down to his long tail, and his front legs were longer than his hind legs.

BRACHIOSAURUS

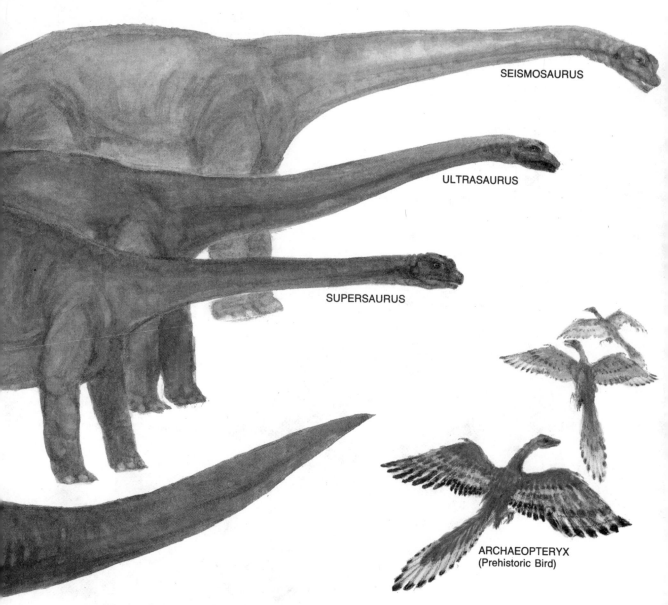

SEISMOSAURUS

ULTRASAURUS

SUPERSAURUS

ARCHAEOPTERYX
(Prehistoric Bird)

Even bigger than Brachiosaurus were Supersaurus and Ultrasaurus. Supersaurus weighed as much as 75 tons and measured 90 feet long. Ultrasaurus weighed up to 135 tons! But scientists now think the biggest dinosaur of all was Seismosaurus, measuring *at least* 110 feet long. No wonder he was given a name which means "earth shaker."

These huge dinosaurs had to eat a lot of food to stay alive. Using their long necks, they could reach up among the tall tree branches for tasty leaves.

Many of the plants we know today did not exist in the time of the dinosaurs. Giant ferns, cone-bearing trees and trees that looked like palm trees grew in damp, hot forests during the early days of the dinosaurs. Later, there were oak, willow and birch trees, plus flowering plants, such as roses. There was plenty of food for the plant-eating dinosaurs.

One group of plant-eaters was the duck-billed dinosaurs. Scientists call them hadrosaurs, and there were many different kinds. One thing they all had in common was a large, flat beak that looked a bit like a duck's bill. The hadrosaurs lived in many parts of the world.

One duck-billed dinosaur was Anatosaurus. This peaceful plant-eater had over 1,000 flat teeth. They were useful for grinding up plants.

Most hadrosaurs had slender front legs and strong back legs. Some had bony crests growing like strange hats on their heads. The purpose of the crests is still a mystery. Because the crests were hollow, some people believe the dinosaurs may have been able to use them to make trumpeting sounds. Or perhaps the crests helped the animals' sense of smell.

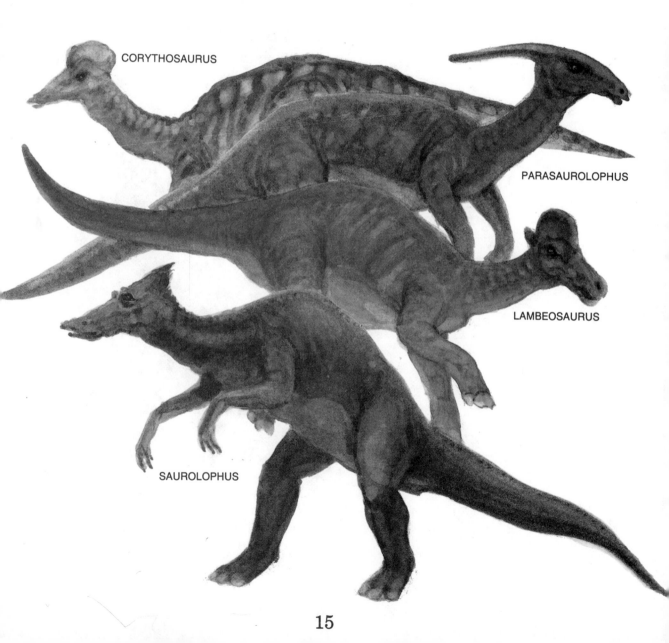

CORYTHOSAURUS

PARASAUROLOPHUS

LAMBEOSAURUS

SAUROLOPHUS

The fierce meat-eaters liked to feast upon the hadrosaurs and other plant-eating dinosaurs. Luckily, some plant-eaters had special ways to defend themselves.

Some duck-billed dinosaurs may have been able to swim out into deep water, where a meat-eater would not follow.

STEGOSAURUS

ANKYLOSAURUS

Other plant-eaters had special weapons for fighting. Ankylosaurus was built like a tank. Short, wide, and very heavy, this dinosaur was covered with flat, thick plates. The plates were very tough. They served as a kind of armor if a meat-eater attacked. Bony spikes also grew along the sides of Ankylosaurus. In battle, this walking tank could swing its heavy, club-like tail at an enemy.

Stegosaurus, a 25-foot-long plant-eater, also had fighting weapons. This animal's tail had a deadly look to it, with two pairs of sharp spikes growing at the end of it. Stegosaurus also had bony plates growing straight up along his neck and back. Some of the plates were two feet high.

But most dinosaurs, no matter how well protected, would not dare to fight the most ferocious dinosaur of all—Tyrannosaurus. This giant, whose name means "tyrant lizard," was feared by plant-eaters.

Towering above many of his victims, the 20-foot-tall monster stood on his back legs. Scientists think that if Tyrannosaurus could run quickly at all, it was only for short distances. He may have waited for his prey to pass. Then, there would be a short chase. This tyrant's front legs were very short and had two sharp claws on them. Worst of all were the six-inch-long teeth of Tyrannosaurus. Like daggers, they tore the flesh of other dinosaurs.

Perhaps the only dinosaur that could meet the challenge of an attacking Tyrannosaurus was Triceratops. This plant-eater was heavier than some kinds of elephants and measured 30 feet long. Its head was enormous and very strong. A bony frill grew around his neck. Triceratops had three sharp horns on his head. Two horns grew above his eyes. The third grew at the end of his nose.

If challenged, Triceratops would charge, stabbing his strong horns into the attacker. That was a threat even Tyrannosaurus took seriously!

Dinosaurs ruled the land millions of years ago. But other prehistoric animals also developed at that time. These unusual creatures became the rulers of the sea and air.

The oceans of long ago were warmer than they are today. They were also not as deep. Racing through these waters, Ichthyosaurs measuring up to 30 feet long would snap at and catch fish to eat.

These sea-going reptiles looked very much like dolphins. And like dolphins, Ichthyosaurs were swift swimmers. They had tall fins, flippers instead of legs, and sharp teeth in their pointed snouts.

A slower ocean dweller was Archelon. At 12 feet long, Archelon was the biggest turtle ever to have lived.

Elasmosaurus, whose name means "thin-plated reptile," had a very long neck that moved about like a ribbon. Paddling slowly through the sea, Elasmosaurus used his neck to jerk his head forward, snatching up fish in his mouth.

ICHTHYOSAUR

ELASMOSAURUS

ARCHELON

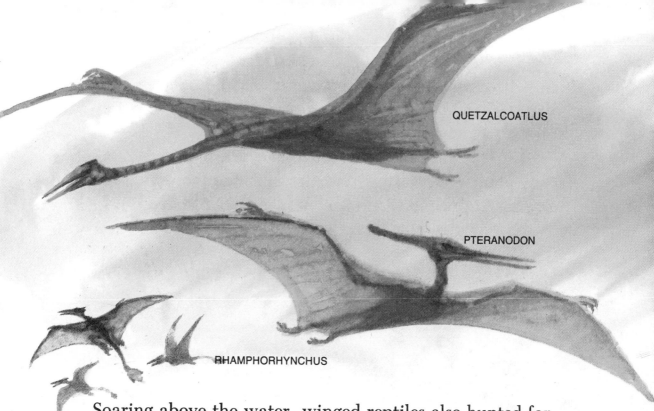

QUETZALCOATLUS

PTERANODON

RHAMPHORHYNCHUS

Soaring above the water, winged reptiles also hunted for fish to eat. One such king of the air was Pteranodon. His wings were 24 feet wide when fully spread. Carried by the wind, Pteranodon would glide along. Then he would swoop down to catch his dinner in his toothless beak.

Quetzalcoatlus was the most monstrous flying reptile of all. His wingspan measured 40 feet across, almost twice the size of Pteranodon's wingspan. What a sight such a creature must have been, as he soared above the open plains of prehistoric time.

A smaller flying reptile was Rhamphorhynchus. He was about 18 inches long. Flapping his wings to fly, rather than gliding, Rhamphorhynchus had large eyes and pointy teeth. This animal may have used his long tail to steer himself through the air.

What happened to the dinosaurs and other prehistoric animals? Once they ruled the world. Then, about 65 million years ago, they died out—they became *extinct.* The reason is still a great mystery.

Did a change in the weather from warm to cool cause many plants to die? If so, the plant-eating dinosaurs would not have enough to eat. They would not be able to live. And if the plant-eaters died out, then the meat-eaters would also starve.

Another theory, or idea, about why the dinosaurs became extinct is that an asteroid, which is a sort of small planet, may have hit the earth. The asteroid would have left a giant dust cloud all around the earth for a long time. If this happened, light could not reach the earth. Plants would die—and without food, so would the dinosaurs.

How do we know about dinosaurs and other prehistoric animals? Our most important information about them comes from fossils. Fossils are the remains and traces of dinosaurs. They can be the bones, teeth, or eggs of dead dinosaurs. Usually, these ancient fossils have been preserved, or saved, in stone through the years.

Some fossils are skin impressions or footprints of these long-ago creatures. Imagine discovering a trail of footprints left by a huge Apatosaurus, as it thundered along millions of years ago!

Paleontologists are the scientists who study dinosaurs and fossils. Often these people find almost-complete skeletons of prehistoric animals. Piece by piece, the bones are carefully chipped out of the earth and stone. Then the skeleton is fitted together, much like a big jigsaw puzzle.

Fossils are wonderful clues to how the dinosaurs looked and lived. For example, the kind of teeth a dinosaur had tells us if the animal ate flesh or plants. The hip and leg bones give us information about whether a dinosaur walked on its hind legs or on all four legs.

Sometimes, paleontologists have discovered 20 or more skeletons of a certain kind of dinosaur all in one place. This suggests that some of the dinosaurs, such as Apatosaurus, lived in big groups called herds.

One important fossil discovery took place in Montana. Scientists there found nests of eggs and baby hadrosaurs, or duck-billed dinosaurs. Nearby, the bodies of adult hadrosaurs were also found. Perhaps the adults were the babies' mothers. Were they caring for the babies and eggs in the nests? Scientists think so.

This fossil find was important because it changed the way scientists think about dinosaurs and their babies. Most reptiles do not care for their young, and that is what was once believed about all dinosaurs. The discovery of the nests seems to show that at least certain kinds of dinosaurs looked after their babies.

Prehistoric animals are fascinating to study. Our imaginary
trip to the days of the dinosaurs has been filled with exciting
creatures and happenings. If you would like to learn more about
dinosaurs, visit a museum. There you will see the skeletons of
these amazing animals.

Study what is left of these enormous animals, and imagine a time when they ruled the earth. These interesting creatures have left behind many unanswered questions. Much about how the dinosaurs lived and why they became extinct is still a mystery. It is a challenging and exciting puzzle that we hope to one day solve.